Basics of Clause and Sentence Structure

Basics of Clause and Sentence Structure

A Handbook for New and Experienced Writers

James R. Wachob

VANTAGE PRESS
New York

Cover design by Susan Thomas

FIRST EDITION

All rights reserved, including the right of
reproduction in whole or in part in any form.

Copyright © 2007 by James R. Wachob

Published by Vantage Press, Inc.
419 Park Ave. South, New York, NY 10016

Manufactured in the United States of America
ISBN: 978-0-533-15634-4

Library of Congress Catalog Card No.: 2006908532

0 9 8 7 6 5 4 3 2 1

To friends I have served as colleague,
teacher, or mentor

Contents

Introduction   ix

Part 1: PUNCTUATION
Punctuation   3

Part 2: CLAUSES
Clauses   11

Part 3: SUBORDINATE CLAUSE REDUCTION
Subordinate Clause Reduction   17

Part 4: SENTENCES
Sentences   25

Part 5: QUIZZES
Quiz No. 1: Punctuation   33
Quiz No. 2: Clauses   35
Quiz No. 3: Subordinate Clause Reduction   37
Quiz No. 4: Sentences   39

ANSWER KEYS
Answer Key No. 1: Punctuation   43
Answer Key No. 2: Clauses   45
Answer Key No. 3: Subordinate Clause Reduction   47
Answer Key No. 4: Sentences   49

Introduction

A wealth of material is available on usage of the individual English parts of speech. At the other extreme of the composition spectrum is an abundance of resources on the production of effective reportage and creative writing. *Basics of Clause and Sentence Structure* fills the gap between those two extremes, which is too often under-stressed in contemporary educational systems, namely, the clause—the fundamental building block in the writing of this and other Western languages.

After a brief review of punctuation marks used, and in some cases to be avoided, in the construction of clauses and sentences, the author describes the categories of clauses. Special attention is given to optional subordinate clause reduction which, when properly employed, can add interest to a piece of writing. Finally, the author describes the categories of sentences resulting from the combining of clauses. Common problems occurring in the construction of clauses and sentences are addressed as dos and don'ts where appropriate.

At the end of the book, a series of quizzes tests the reader's grasp of the material presented. Explanatory answer keys aid in the learning process.

Basics of Clause and Sentence Structure reflects six decades of the author's writing experience in the military, diplomacy, and academia, all fields in which the avoidance of distracting or potentially misleading errors in written clause and sentence structure assumed major importance.

Basics of Clause and Sentence Structure

Part 1

PUNCTUATION

Punctuation

Period

A period is used to end a declarative sentence.

The meeting was constructive.

A period is used in decimal notation.

They drove 31.5 miles to the beach.

Question Mark

A question mark is used to end an interrogative sentence.

Who invited him?

Exclamation Mark

An exclamation mark is used to end an expression of surprise or a command.

She finished the hour-long test in only 30 minutes!

Close the door!

Semicolon

A semicolon is used to separate two main clauses not joined by a conjunction.

> The house burned down; it was the final blow to the family.

A semicolon is used to separate two main clauses joined by a conjunctive adverb (e.g., **therefore, however, nevertheless**). The conjunctive adverb must be preceded by a semicolon and followed by a comma.

> The funds are inadequate; therefore, the program must be discontinued.

Comma

A comma is used to separate main clauses joined by a coordinating conjunction (**and, but, or, nor, for, so, yet**).

> Almost everyone knows how to earn money, but not everyone knows how to spend it well.

[The comma may be omitted between two short main clauses.]

> She forgot her jacket so she caught cold.

A comma is used to separate words, phrases, and clauses in a series of three or more items.

> The country's chief agricultural products are potatoes, cabbage, and beets.

[In a series of three or more items, the comma may be omitted before **and** and before **or** if the omission would not interfere with clarity of meaning. The final comma should not be omitted in the following sentence.]

> For breakfast he ordered orange juice, toast and butter, and bacon and eggs.

A comma is used to set off a long introductory phrase or a subordinate clause from the rest of the sentence.

> Having rid themselves of their former rulers, the people now disagreed on the new leadership.

> Although the details of the plan are not clear, we should proceed as quickly as possible.

A comma is often used to set off an introductory modifying word or phrase to improve the readability of a sentence.

> Overjoyed, she telephoned her parents the good news.

> Silently and swiftly, the police surrounded the building.

Commas are used to set off a non-restrictive adjective clause. [Commas are <u>not</u> used to set off a restrictive adjective clause.]

Mr. Jones, who is the boss, lives near the factory.

Commas are used to set off an appositive.

Mr. Jones, the boss, lives near the factory.

Commas are used to set off conjunctive adverbs and parenthetical expressions.

The use of pesticides, however, has its disadvantages.

You may, if you wish, demand a refund.

Colon

A colon is used to introduce a series of items.

The three committees are as follows: membership, finance, and nominations.

A colon is used to indicate that an initial clause will be further explained or illustrated by the material that follows the colon.

It was a city notorious for its inadequacies: its schools were antiquated, its administration was corrupt, and everyone felt the burden of its taxes.

Common Writing Errors

- Remember that in American English, commas and periods are placed inside the quotation marks.

    "Hello, Bob", said Mary, "I'm happy to see you". [not U.S. style]
    "Hello, Bob," said Mary, "I'm happy to see you."

- Remember to use the exclamation mark sparingly. Overuse of the exclamation mark lessens its emphatic effect.

    The beaches were sandy! The food was great! I want to go back! [devaluation of the exclamation mark]

- Remember that a period, not a comma, is used in decimal notation.

    The bottle contained 25,3 fluid ounces. [not U.S. style]

    The bottle contained 25.3 fluid ounces.

Part 2

CLAUSES

Clauses

Definition

A clause consists of one or more subjects of one or more verbs and may include one or more direct objects, one or more indirect objects, and one or more modifiers, e.g., adjectives, adverbs and adverbial phrases, prepositional phrases, and infinitive phrases. Each of the following is one clause:

<u>Mary is sleeping.</u>
<u>John gave us his book.</u>
<u>Susan and Bill are singing and dancing.</u>
<u>The dark-haired woman wanted very much to walk to the store yesterday.</u>
<u>Before the class started this morning. . . .</u>
<u>. . . after the football game ended.</u>

Categories of Clauses

There are two principal categories of clauses:

Main (Independent) Clauses

A main clause is any clause that can be ended with a

period, question mark, exclamation mark, or semicolon. It can be followed by a comma only (a) if the comma is followed by a coordinating conjunction (**and, but, for, nor, or, so, yet**) and by another main clause; or (b) if the main clause is one of three or more main classes in a series.

<u>They enjoy skiing.</u>
<u>Where is Sam?</u>
<u>The world's biggest diamond has been stolen!</u>
<u>Bob likes cake; Jane prefers cookies.</u>
<u>He has three hobbies: painting, stamp-collecting, and hang-gliding.</u>
<u>We'll arrive in Chicago at noon, and we'll check in at the Grand Hotel.</u>
<u>She's working hard, she's earning a good salary, and she's saving to buy a car.</u>

<u>Subordinate (Dependent) Clauses</u>

A subordinate clause is a clause that cannot be followed by a period, question mark, exclamation mark, or semicolon.

- An <u>adjective</u> clause (also called a relative clause), which usually begins with **who, whom, whose, which, where, when,** or **that**, describes a person, animal, place, thing, or concept.

  A <u>restrictive</u> adjective clause provides information essential for identifying the referenced noun, pronoun, or gerund. A restrictive adjective clause is not enclosed within commas. It often begins with **that, who, whom, whose, which,** or **when**.

I will visit my brother <u>who lives in New York.</u>
 [I have more than one brother; the others live elsewhere.]
I have two sisters. The sister <u>who speaks Spanish</u> lives in Spain.

A <u>non-restrictive</u> adjective clause provides unessential information related to the referenced noun, pronoun, or gerund. A non-restrictive adjective clause is enclosed within commas. It often begins with **who, whom, whose, which, where,** or **when**.

I will visit my brother, <u>who lives in New York.</u>
 [I have only one brother.]
This book, <u>which was written by my friend,</u> was expensive.

- An <u>adverb</u> clause describes the time, cause and effect, opposition, or condition of an action or state.

 <u>Before the class started,</u> the teacher called the roll.
 <u>Because Mary forgot her book,</u> she had to borrow one from the library.
 <u>Although it was raining,</u> we walked in the park.
 <u>If the bus doesn't come soon,</u> they'll be late for school.

An adverb clause preceding a main clause is followed by a comma.

> If the weather is good, we'll play football

A main clause preceding an adverb clause is normally not followed by a comma. However, a comma is often used when the adverb clause begins with an adverb of opposition (**although, even though, though, whereas, while**).

> We'll play football after school is out.
> We'll play football, even though it's going to snow.

- A noun clause can serve as a subject or direct object. A noun clause often begins with **that, what, whoever,** and **whomever**.

> That Patricia is ill is very unfortunate.
> I don't understand what the boss said.

A noun clause can also serve as the object of a preposition.

> The prize will be given to whoever wins the race.
> *The prize will be given to whomever wins the race.* [ungrammatical]
> The prize will be given to whomever we select.

Common Writing Errors

- No adjective clause can begin with **what**.

- No non-restrictive adjective clause can begin with **that**.

Part 3

SUBORDINATE CLAUSE REDUCTION

Subordinate Clause Reduction

Adjective (Relative) Clauses

a. When the relative pronoun serves as the <u>subject</u> and precedes the verb **to be**, the clause can often be reduced by eliminating the relative pronoun (**that, which, who**) and the verb **to be**, if the subordinate clause contains a prepositional phrase, a progressive verb, or a passive verb. Reduction can also occur if the subordinate clause is <u>non-restrictive</u> and contains a predicate nominative or a predicate adjective; reduction cannot occur if the subordinate clause is <u>restrictive</u> and contains a predicate nominative or a predicate adjective. [A predicate nominative is a noun or noun clause following the verb **to be**; a predicate adjective is an adjective following the verb **to be**.]

ORIGINAL: The house **that is** on the corner belongs to my sister.
REDUCED: The house on the corner belongs to my sister. [restrictive sub. clause with prepositional phrase]

ORIGINAL: Bill's car, **which is** still in the garage, was in a big accident.
REDUCED: Bill's car, still in the garage, was in a big accident. [non-restrictive sub. clause with prepositional phrase]

ORIGINAL: The girl **who is** studying here is my cousin.
REDUCED: The girl studying here is my cousin. [restrictive sub. clause with progressive verb]

ORIGINAL: Mr. Smith, **who was** driving too fast, received a ticket.
REDUCED: Mr. Smith, driving too fast, received a ticket. [non-restrictive sub. clause with progressive verb]

ORIGINAL: The street **that was** paved yesterday carries a lot of traffic.
REDUCED: The street paved yesterday carries a lot of traffic. [restrictive sub. clause with passive verb]

ORIGINAL: Mary's cookies, **which were** baked this morning, will be given to the children.
REDUCED: Mary's cookies, baked this morning, will be given to the children. [non-restrictive sub. clause with passive verb]

ORIGINAL: The official **who is** the most important person in the city is the mayor.
INCORRECT: *The official the most important person in the city is the mayor. [restrictive sub. clause with predicate nominative; reduction not possible]*

ORIGINAL: Dr. Thompson, who is a professor, lives in California.

REDUCED:	Dr. Thompson, a professor, lives in California. [non-restrictive sub. clause with predicate nominative]
ORIGINAL:	The flower **that was** the most beautiful in the contest was an orchid.
INCORRECT:	*The flower the most beautiful in the contest was an orchid. [restrictive sub. clause with predicate adjective; reduction not possible]*
ORIGINAL:	Paul, **who was** better trained than the others, won the race.
REDUCED:	Paul, better trained than the others, won the race. [non-restrictive sub. clause with predicate adjective]

b. When the relative pronoun serves as the <u>direct object,</u> a restrictive adjective clause can be reduced by eliminating the relative pronoun (**that, which, whom**). If the adjective clause is <u>non-restrictive,</u> reduction is not possible.

ORIGINAL:	The dress **that** Mary bought is expensive.
REDUCED:	The dress Mary bought is expensive.
ORIGINAL:	The woman **whom** he married is a friend of mine.
REDUCED:	The woman he married is a friend of mine.

Adverb Clauses

When an adverb clause (a) begins with an expression of time, condition, or opposition, and (b) contains the verb **to be**, the clause can often be reduced by eliminating the subject and the verb **to be**. Reduction is possible only if the subject of the main clause can serve as the subject of the reduction.

ORIGINAL: When **it was** newly invented, the telephone seemed like a miracle.
REDUCED: When newly invented, the telephone seemed like a miracle. [expression of time]

ORIGINAL: If **they are** too worn down, your tires should be replaced.
REDUCED: If too worn down, your tires should be replaced. [expression of condition]

ORIGINAL: Although **he was** poor, the old man still dressed quite well.
REDUCED: Although poor, the old man still dressed quite well. [expression of opposition]

ORIGINAL: Because **they were** so excited, they couldn't fall asleep.
INCORRECT: *Because so excited, they couldn't fall asleep.* [Reduction is not possible when the adverb clause begins with an adverb of cause and effect (e.g., **because, since, now that**).]

ORIGINAL: While **we were** swimming, our dinner was being prepared.
INCORRECT: *While swimming, our dinner was being prepared.* [Reduction is not possible because the subject of the main clause is not the subject of the reduction.]

Noun Clauses

a. When a noun clause beginning with **that** serves as the <u>direct object</u> in another clause, **that** can be eliminated.

ORIGINAL: They thought **that** it was getting late.
REDUCED: They thought it was getting late.

b. When a noun clause beginning with **that** serves as a <u>predicate nominative</u> in another clause, **that** can be eliminated. [A predicate nominative is a noun or noun clause following the verb **to be**.]

ORIGINAL: My hope is **that** you'll call me tomorrow.
REDUCED: My hope is you'll call me tomorrow.

Placement of Reduced Subordinate Clauses

A reduced adjective (relative) clause or adverb clause can remain between the subject and verb of the main clause. However, it is common in writing for the reduced clause to be removed to the beginning of the sentence.

ORIGINAL: The student, **who was pleased with the result**, gave his essay to the teacher.

REDUCED: The student, **pleased with the result**, gave his essay to the teacher.
REMOVED: **Pleased with the result**, the student gave his essay to the teacher.

ORIGINAL: The man, **although he was injured**, still fought the robbers.
REDUCED: The man, **although injured**, still fought the robbers.
REMOVED: **Although injured**, the man still fought the robbers.

Part 4

SENTENCES

Sentences

Note: MC = main (independent) clause
MC/S = main clause subject
MC/V = main clause verb
SC = subordinate (dependent) clause
CC = coordinating conjunction
CA = conjunctive adverb

Every sentence must have at least one main clause.

Simple Sentences

If the main clause stands alone with proper punctuation, the structure is a simple sentence.

Our friends went to the theater.

In addition to one main clause, a sentence may have one or more additional main clauses and one or more subordinate clauses.

Compound Sentences

A main clause can be combined with other main clauses in four ways to produce a compound sentence.

- With a coordinating conjunction (**and, but, for, nor, or, so, yet**)

  Most students have good study habits, but others do not.
  [MC, CC MC]

- With a semicolon

  Most students have good study habits; others do not.
  [MC; MC]

- With a conjunctive adverb (e.g., **therefore, however, nevertheless**)

  Most students have good study habits; however, others do not.
  [MC; CA, MC]

- With a coordinating conjunction preceding the second main clause, which is inserted (within commas) between the subject of the first main clause and the verb of the first main clause.

  Many students, and they are in the majority, have good study habits.
  [MC/S, CC MC, MC/V]

Complex Sentences

A main clause can be combined with one or more subordinate clauses in three ways to produce a complex sentence.

- With the main clause preceded by the subordinate clause

  Although many students have good study habits, some do not.
  [SC, MC]

- With the main clause followed by the subordinate clause

  Some students have good study habits although others do not.
  [MC SC]

- With the subordinate clause inserted (within commas) between the subject of the main clause and the verb of the main clause

  Most students, if they have good study habits, will pass the course.
  [MC/S, SC, MC/V]

In the last of the three foregoing structures, it is important that the subordinate clause [SC] not be replaced by a main clause [MC]. If the subordinate clause contains a preposition followed by a pronoun, the pronoun must be either **whom** (for people) or **which** (for everything else). Following the preposition with either **that** or a personal pronoun (**me, you, him, her, it, us, them**) would have the ungrammatical result of converting the subordinate clause [SC] into a main clause [MC].

- There were three houses on the street, the largest of **which** was brown.
  [MC, SC]

  *There were three houses on the street, the largest of **them** was brown.*
  [MC, MC] ungrammatical

- The doctors, some of **whom** speak French, have Canadian patients.
  [MC/S, SC, MC/V]

  *The doctors, some of **them** speak French, have Canadian patients.*
  [MC/S, MC, MC/V] ungrammatical

- The puppies, all of **which** ran away yesterday, have been found.
  [MC/S, SC, MC/V]

  *The puppies, all of **them** ran away yesterday, have been found.*
  [MC/S, MC, MC/V] ungrammatical

Common Writing Errors

- Avoid "run-on" sentences. Unless three or more main clauses are in a series, do not allow one main clause to follow another main clause without a coordinating conjunction.

Margaret likes to swim, Robert doesn't like to swim.
   [MC, MC] ungrammatical

- Avoid "sentence fragments." Unless a structure contains at least one main clause, it cannot end with a period, question mark, exclamation mark, or semicolon.

Because the roads were icy and very dangerous that day.
   [SC] ungrammatical

- Avoid confusion when a main clause, such as "we believe" or "everybody knew," is inserted into another clause:

  a. when inserted between the <u>subject</u> and <u>verb</u> of another clause

  This is the candidate **who** we believe <u>should be elected</u>.
  [**whom** is never acceptable in this case]

  b. When inserted between the <u>object</u> and the <u>subject</u> of another clause

  This is the candidate **whom** we believe <u>the voters</u> should elect.
  [**who** is acceptable in some editorial circles]

Part 5

QUIZZES

Quiz No. 1: Punctuation

Mark (X) for any incorrect statement below and be prepared to explain your answer.

    ____1. Because the water was so warm we had a good time at the beach.

    ____2. Bill likes basketball, Juan prefers soccer.

    ____3. They wanted to see the movie, but they didn't have enough money.

    ____4. The women were too tired to walk, therefore they took a taxi.

    ____5. "I'm happy", said the substitute teacher, "to be with you today".

    ____6. Last summer was very hot and humid in our city; so we often went to the swimming pool.

    ____7. Prices keep rising, but wages often don't rise as fast.

    ____8. Mary is a teacher, Sally is a nurse, Susan manages a restaurant.

____9. Wherever they are in this city.

____10. Paul, who is my only brother, lives in Chicago.

Quiz No. 2: Clauses

Mark (X) for any incorrect statement below and be prepared to explain your answer.

____1. My mother, who is a teacher, lives in Texas.

____2. We'll drive to the mountains this weekend if it doesn't snow.

____3. What the doctor announced, was good news.

____4. A picture will be painted by whomever wins the competition.

____5. My very best friend who is also my neighbor is in my class.

____6. Whomever the students elect will be the next class president.

____7. The book what I bought yesterday is an interesting novel.

____8. The yellow house, that was built last year, belongs to a rich man.

____9. A bonus will be given to whoever has the best work record this month.

____10. That necklace, which is the most beautiful one in the store, costs a fortune.

Quiz No. 3: Subordinate Clause Reduction

Mark (X) for any incorrect statement and be prepared to explain your answer.

____1. The man is walking with his sons are a banker.

____2. Flying over the city, the buildings looked very small.

____3. The students, impressed by the visiting lecturer, asked for her autograph.

____4. Written in Spanish, the student could understand the letter.

____5. Sitting alone in the park, the fish were being fed by the old man.

____6. The horses running in tomorrow's race are among the best in the state.

____7. The speech given by the governor outlined his plans for new hospitals.

____8. The wild animal was trapped last week had rabies.

____9. Houses built fifty years ago often need their electrical systems upgraded.

____10. Happy about his good grades, the boy gave his report card to his parents.

Quiz No. 4: Sentences

Mark (X) for any incorrect statement below and be prepared to explain your answer.

____1. The beautiful forest, which covered the entire mountainside.

____2. A good friend if you have one is a very special person in your life.

____3. Five musical instruments, the oldest of which was made 100 years ago, were used for last night's chamber music concert.

____4. There were fifty graduating seniors, the youngest of them was only 16.

____5. New York is an exciting city, Chicago is also a popular tourist destination.

____6. Mr. Jones is the person who everyone thinks should be the next governor.

____7. My father, who is employed in a small company, enjoys his work.

_____ 8. This is the girl whom most students believe is going to be the next Festival Queen.

_____ 9. Traffic tickets are given to whoever drives above the speed limit in our town.

_____ 10. A prize will be awarded to the artist who submits the best painting.

ANSWER KEYS

Answer Key No. 1: Punctuation

1. Incorrect. When it precedes a main clause, a subordinate clause must be followed by a comma. "Because the water was so warm, we had a good time at the beach."

2. Incorrect. Two main clauses cannot be joined only by a comma. "Bill likes basketball, but Juan prefers soccer." Or "Bill likes basketball; Juan prefers soccer."

3. Correct.

4. Incorrect. When two main clauses are joined by a conjunctive adverb ("therefore"), the conjunctive adverb must be preceded by a semicolon and followed by a comma. "The women were too tired to walk; therefore, they took a taxi."

5. Incorrect. In the United States, quotation marks are placed after commas and periods. "I'm happy," said the substitute teacher, "to be with you today."

6. Incorrect. Two main clauses can be joined either by a semicolon or by a coordinating conjunction but not by both. "Last summer was very hot and humid in our city, so we often went to the swimming pool." Or

"Last summer was very hot and humid in our city; we often went to the swimming pool."

7. Correct.

8. Incorrect. When three or more main clauses are joined together, the last one must be preceded by a comma and a coordinating conjunction. "Mary is a teacher, Sally is a nurse, and Susan manages a restaurant."

9. Incorrect. Because there is no main clause, the statement cannot end with a period. A main clause can be placed at the beginning of the subordinate clause: "Tourists can find good restaurants wherever they are in this city." Or a main clause can be placed at the end of the subordinate clause: "Wherever they are in this city, tourists can find good restaurants."

10. Correct.

Answer Key No. 2: Clauses

1. Correct.

2. Correct.

3. Incorrect. The subject is a noun clause serving as the subject of the verb "was." A subject cannot be separated from its verb by a single comma. "What the doctor announced was good news."

4. Incorrect. The subject of the verb "wins" must be "whoever." "A picture will be painted by whoever wins the competition."

5. Incorrect. You have only one "very best friend," so the adjective (relative) clause is non-restrictive. That clause should therefore be enclosed within commas. "My very best friend, who is also my neighbor, is in my class."

6. Correct.

7. Incorrect. "What" can never begin an adjective (relative) clause. "The book that I bought yesterday is an interesting novel."

8. Incorrect. "That was built last year" is enclosed in

commas and is therefore a non-restrictive adjective (relative) clause. A non-restrictive clause cannot begin with "that." If the commas are removed, the clause becomes a restrictive clause, and "that" would therefore be correct.

9. Correct.

10. Correct.

Answer Key No. 3: Subordinate Clause Reduction

1. Incorrect. The subject of the main clause "man" must have a singular verb. "The man walking with his sons is a banker." Or "The man who is walking with his sons is a banker."

2. Incorrect. The subject of the main clause "buildings" cannot be the subject of the reduction. "Flying over the city, we thought the buildings looked very small."

3. Correct.

4. Incorrect. The subject of the main clause "student" cannot be the subject of the reduction. "Written in Spanish, the letter could be understood by the student."

5. Incorrect. The subject of the main clause "fish" cannot be the subject of the reduction. "Sitting alone in the park, the old man was feeding the fish."

6. Correct.

7. Correct.

8. Incorrect. The sentence can be changed to include a

reduction: "The wild animal trapped last week had rabies." The sentence can also be expanded to include an adjective (relative) clause: "The wild animal that was trapped last week had rabies."

9. Correct.

10. Correct.

Answer Key No. 4: Sentences

1. Incorrect. The subject "forest" has no verb. The sentence could be corrected by adding a verb and additional language, if desired. "The beautiful forest, which covered the entire mountainside, was a national park."

2. Incorrect. If one clause is inserted between the subject and verb of another clause, the inserted clause must be enclosed within commas. "A good friend, if you have one, is a very special person in your life."

3. Correct.

4. Incorrect. Two main clauses are joined by a comma with no coordinating conjunction. The sentence can be corrected by changing the second clause into an adjective (relative) clause. "There were fifty graduating seniors, the youngest of whom was only 16."

5. Incorrect. Two main clauses are joined by a comma with no coordinating conjunction. The sentence can be corrected by inserting a coordinating conjunction (e.g., **and, but**) before the subject of the second clause. "New York is an exciting city, and Chicago is also a popular tourist destination." The sentence can also be corrected by changing the comma to a semico-

lon. "New York is an exciting city; Chicago is also a popular tourist destination."

6. Correct.

7. Correct.

8. Incorrect. This sentence has three clauses. The first is "This is the girl." The second clause is "most students believe." The third clause has the verb "is going to be," which requires a subject; "whom" can never serve as a subject. The sentence should be corrected to read: "This is the girl who most students believe is going to be the next Festival Queen."

9. Correct.

10. Correct.